The Sign for Water

Previous publication: *Light from the Upper Left* (with Bob Cooper), Smith/Doorstop Books 1994 (joint winner of The Poetry Business Competition 1993).

Acknowledgements are due to Lancaster Literary Festival; Lincoln Poetry Competition; *The North*; *Stand*.

The Sign for Water

Jo Haslam

Smith/Doorstop Books

Published 1998 by
Smith/Doorstop Books
The Poetry Business
The Studio
Byram Arcade
Westgate
Huddersfield HD1 1ND

Copyright © Jo Haslam
All Rights Reserved

ISBN 1 869961 83 8

British Library Cataloguing-in-Publication Data. A catalogue record for this book is available from the British Library.

Jo Haslam hereby asserts her moral right to be identified as the author of this book.

Typeset at The Poetry Business
Printed by Peepal Tree Press, Leeds

Distributed by Password (Books) Ltd.,
2 Little Peter Street, Manchester M15 4PS

The Poetry Business acknowledges the help of Kirklees Metropolitan Council and Yorkshire & Humberside Arts.

Cover design by Luke Haslam

CONTENTS

7	The September Swimmer
8	The Shape of the Heart
10	Snow
11	Diving Bell
13	Journey to Crown Court
14	Fox-stopped
15	CEO 262
16	Riddle
17	Homecoming
18	Double Crown
19	Proof
20	The Faithful Dog
21	Closing
22	Your First Black Hair
23	Crooning
25	Charms
26	The Risen Man
27	Allergies
28	Dos-à-Dos
29	Hindi Urdu Bol Chaal
30	Lost
31	Gibson Copy
32	Inheritance
33	When the Moon is Orange
34	Geronimo
35	Birds Fly South
37	Icarus
38	Vincent Writes to Theo from the North
39	Proofs
40	Odalisque
41	Wide Open
42	My Father's Teeth
44	Six Foot
45	Early Warning
47	Each Star is a Sun
48	Lagoon
49	Sunburn
50	Test

51	Mr Wrong
52	Betrayal
53	The Sign For Water
55	Sign Language
57	Collector
58	Fluke
59	One Man and his Dog
60	Night Swimmers

The September Swimmer

In September moorhens
reclaim the quiet water
at the deepest stretch, where the canal divides
and one part broadens into a reservoir.
Trees thicken on one side, and on the other
fields slope up to lonely farms.

Trippers come here on hot days, paddling dinghies,
scattering paper cups and sandwich wrappers,
leaving car doors open or banging them
and playing radios. Children race each other
down the shallow sand bank and some
simply sunbathe. But in autumn

the water sinks back into silence.
Only the weather disturbs it, or fishermen
and one solitary swimmer, who comes each evening
before dusk and slides white limbs
from the coping stones with hardly a splash.
Her body flattens in the water and flickers greenly

as she kicks from one side to the other.
She swims steadily not seeming to notice
if it's cold or how the dark slips up
earlier each night. She moves
past the broken tree root and the sandbank
touches the side and, hardly pausing, turns.

She seems as integral to the water
as the steady rise and fall of hills
are to the landscape, and I imagine her
gliding through October mists and into winter
setting perfect formalised patterns
like those made by moorhens; link after link

of sliding circles that spread and in
the cold deep centre form a body-shaped space,
solid rings of water that follow the contours
of arms, torso, head; fossilised till the cold breaks.
Each day of winter that I pass, I think I hear
the crack of her surfacing through ice.

The Shape of the Heart

To feed us up your mother cooks for us,
cow-heel stew, calf's head broth, black puddings, heart.
I poke at it suspicious and confirmed
in everything I thought of the barbaric north.
But not being vegetarian I have to eat.
The pieces that curl from her knife –
roughly the shape convention has made perfect –
are close textured and you say surprisingly sweet.
I cut mine into quarters, eighths, deliberately
as if dissecting atria and ventricle,
artery and vein, fixing the names like the diagrams
we drew at school, but nothing like
the heart your mother has made edible
and even less the wild thumping heart of the animal.
What shape is that? The shape that fits the hand,
the heart dilated, its furious departure from the norm
set off by the sharp smack on the rump;
then the squealing fear, smell of blood,
the hand when it's done pulling out
guts and liver, lungs, heart, fingers closing round
the veined and bulbous, the dangerous scarlet
or darker crimson that's still nothing like the heart
that we expect. This heart's become
a rust red glove and is still so far from
the one we colour unblemished;
the engraved, embossed, the silky pincushion
the unequivocally symmetrical. The heart
much more various, erratic and unfinished
– like the letter signed –
the scribbled desperate card – my love you are breaking my –
what shape is that? The heart on the sleeve
the heart crossed, the heart you're hardly aware of
unless it quickens or misses a beat,
the heart that's made by how we shape our lives
though some would say it's the other way about.
The heart that sounds alone in the night impossibly loud.
The heart the shape of grief, lies, hate, the loving
and the passionate, the shape of countries,
seas, exile, the hospital chart,

the electrocardiograph, the heart you say
you can read, the heart you desire
intact, unique, no counterfeit, no fake –
in short the perfect heart.
But the heart you ask of me
is no shape I can predict, already encumbered,
incomplete; the heart I offer now, the heart you take,
for this moment and this place, on this heart I draw your face.

Snow

It was the slightest touch against his shoulder
that made him turn. Snow, coming from behind,
cold January, a heavy sky.
She saw the shoulders of his tweed
sports jacket, powdered white.
A crystal blurring on his lashes
as he looked up and said
'More to come tonight.'

Already it was thickening
blowing round their heads and deadening every noise,
except their voices calling through drifting flakes.
If she'd known then the cold that would reach out to him
she'd have shouted till her heart burst,
unfrozen him with quick warm breath
as she had blown away so easily the snow
that settled on his mouth and eyelids.

But they have altered the shape of his mouth,
packed his flesh hard white.
She can't make a sound. Cold has set inside her,
a stone of ice nothing can melt.

Diving Bell

I thought of them, the four little ones who died
while sailing out to India, that year,
just before the war; small packages
swaddled, sealed and slipped overboard.
That one was your mother's story.

Or your father bringing
his brother out of the water, not dead quite
but changed. He never could get over
that white face, the closed pebble-veined eyes;
and always, when looked at from the side,
that queer iridescence.

Then in Ireland, one holiday,
a whole boatload gone down.
On the harbour an absolute quiet
as they waited for the news.
Your aunt in the kitchen just before.
The slap of dough on the board,
a film of flour dusting her hands.

And it came back, St Martin's Eve
when eighty men were drowned –
whole families and friends.
All these when hearing of the ship
that foundered in the dark, and the men
inside the diving bell
that came to rest on the ocean floor.
The story was in the papers for days
until there was no hope
of finding anyone alive.

I thought of all that weight of ocean,
strange plant life, unknown pollution,
the cold indifferent salt water,
and none of it for certain could corrode
the sealed room that held those seven men,
dead drowned divers, under the dark sea
that closed above the diving bell.

No strangers there, they'd known the different
movements, weight; could compute
the pressure on each square inch,
how deep the water and how strange,
how uncertain their tenure –
this too, just like the first breath-holding divers
who risked deafness, sometimes their lives
plunging for pearl or sponge.

And we as much as they are divers still,
resume what was our element as aliens –
observers, predators, lovers too.
We trawl sea depths where sunlight
never reaches, reefs of coral,
fish that lose colour as they swim deeper,
to close at last on treasures, miracles of pearl
and surface, or fall and fall into the ocean.

Journey to Crown Court

Going there you fell asleep, head to one side.
Your face had that bleached look
of one who was very tired, or ill.
But you slept, almost as if
you were entering a period of recovery.

We in the front seats couldn't think ahead
only about now,
how many miles to go before our destination
newspapers we'd left behind,
small change for parking ...

I watched you in the mirror.
You'd slept like this before, rocked
by the motion of a train or car.
At those journeys' ends I'd lift you on my shoulder,
your body solid and hot, skin like a crumpled petal.

Now you unfold long limbs, ease your legs
from the back seat, shake your trouser crease,
look up, it's raining, cold drops
out of the morning sky, blotching the street.
At the door, going in, no time for goodbye,
you stopped, just once, suddenly to kiss me and I
began to cry.

Fox-stopped

I thought of how we stopped for the fox
that night coming back from the coast;
how in the headlights his eyes shone,
a sudden brilliance before he swerved
and plunged into the dark moor drop.
We hadn't heard the thud like that dog once
that leapt out in the road at dusk,
we didn't see him thrown up in the air, explode,
but certain that we'd caught him searched
each slope up or downwards from the road.

I see us still, my hand stretched out to part the bracken,
peering through the moonless dark
and you just twelve and running
with all your twelve years' speed and passion.
'No use', I said, 'to chase him if he's hurt.'
though we still searched. And look!
it's just as though you were still running.
And listen! now I can't tell if what I hear
is my heart beating or your pounding feet.
Five years and you've brought us here, fox-stopped.
Except that you're the fox now, hunted, stunned,
and I'm feeling for you in the dark.

CEO 262

Take nothing dear to you
it will be lost or stolen.
Take nothing that you value,
six paperback books,
a cheap watch,
the clothes you stand up in.

Take no toothbrush, soap,
no scissors, knife or medicine,
no photograph of yourself.
You will be washed,
hair and nails cut,
your clothes taken from you.

Nights you will wake up,
reach for the things you love
but you will find strange cloth
next to your skin, your fingers brush
a bare table top. All those things
dear to you stolen or lost.

And if I could
then I would clothe you, but
my dear you must go naked.
So be vigilant, take on
protective colouring, learn
to look behind you when you walk.

And count them in your sleep
the things you thought were stolen, two pearls
which are milk teeth, a ring
of woven hair, a half moon cut
from a thumb nail. Men have been saved
by lesser charms than these.

Riddle

What was it that you were?
You were all of these things:
You were a fragile face I had
to hold between my hands
to stop it from disintegrating.
You were a boy with sunlight
on his flaky skin.
You were a terrible deep wound.
You were someone I could confuse
with someone else,
a man whose stomach troubled him.
You were a baby who would not stop crying.

You were very small, hard as a pebble.
You were larva soft, you were tall
then small again, tall with a flapping coat
dark with a white skin, your hands were cold.
You were someone like my brother
or my child. You were the one
I could never write about.

Now, I cloak you in words.
They print your skin like kisses,
crosses, thin as tissue, as my pen,
they fold, stroke the bruised
dark patch below your eyes,
they link your dry cold hands with mine.

You are that one, the heavy weight inside,
the leaf-like nervous flutter
where my stomach hollowed.

And in each case you are an ache,
a fragile face, a boy
with flaky skin, short sighted,
someone like my brother
or my son, a child who in the night
I am still listening for,
a baby who will not stop crying.

Homecoming

I thought when I woke that you were there.
I thought you'd lean forward
from the back seat of the car
and put your arms around me.
I thought I'd brought you home.

Sometimes walking on the road
I think I'll turn and you'll be with me.
Sometimes it's as though I catch you
at the corner of my eye.
Sometimes I almost touch your coat.

The black one that swings out behind.
And I recognise your shape,
that stride, but it's always
someone else, I understand
that phrase now, 'my heart in my mouth'.

Mine's everywhere, it seems to jump,
alter its size – sometimes large
an awful weight or fast and light,
or else it's gone or else I think
it's broken. But it still knocks

and then I know its exact location,
when it's quiet, night time, my door
opens with a rush of air. And I look up
with sudden hope that it's you coming in
moisture on your coat and hair.

Double Crown

You have a double crown, which makes your hair
difficult to cut. I thought it would be easier
the second growth, but there was always
more of it, soft light brown, and though
I started carefully I'd find myself
cutting more and more, as though by cutting it
I could reach back to the first close swirls.

I could see the way it grew then, how it balanced
the large features, how it lifted from the scalp
and fell – as if you'd grown backwards
to the original hard and awkward head.

You know the body, skin, blood cells, renew
themselves continually. Hair, skin flakes,
fall without us noticing. But I
am paring you back through all of these renewals
to the definite line of the skull, and the hair
is falling like blossom, light and casual.

Proof

The smell of you is on your clothes
even though they have been washed
and folded in the drawer
since you've been away.

Your brother took a shirt out the other day
and wears it now continually.
The cuffs hang down below his wrists
the hemline to his knees. He says
you gave him permission. Your jacket,
shirts, sweaters that are probably
too small. When he is at school
I wash them. Arms and chest billow
on the line and still the smell of you clings,
much more strongly to the wool
than to your other clothes.

De-pilling them,
I gathered up the little matted tufts
and rolled them in a ball, forgot them
till the cat discovered one and chased it
without warning, pounced, and we
all jumped, thinking it was something else
just like the time when someone knocked:
the door flew open suddenly,
my head jerked up,
my heart almost stopped.

The Faithful Dog

You look for your dog to stay faithful.
Imagine how his ears prick up
when you walk in,
his whine and his excited scratching at the door.

You look for everything to be
just as you left it,
drawings undisturbed, no dust. Your books,
one still face down, open on the floor.

You look for faces turned towards you
your lover's a white blur
as she runs across the room. But you
have come out of a cold dream

amazed to feel your face
glistened with sweat.
You dreamed you had come back
come home, to find everything different

the house changed, although you lift
your hand to knock, hear
the dog that you thought faithful
growl a warning low down in his throat.

His eyesight's faded; he's too old
to recognise you.
And you are grown so much taller
wearing such strange clothes.

Closing

This door closes with a shudder of glass
loose inside the frame; another jams
with the swelling of cheap new wood
and this much older one settles in its groove,
wood worn into wood.
Your door wouldn't close without a push.

Inside the windows shook
and the door echoed, but all doors echo
with the sound of rooms they close on.
Yours is different now.
You say there is a final clanging sound
– the noise that comes from hard surfaces.

If I could I would send back another sound.
Unlock doors for you. You'd step out
into the summer night, no traffic on the road,
the hum of heat just damping down
and something calling, bat or owl.
Or when it's very cold, the hush before snow

and after it's fallen the difference
in the noise your footstep makes. Invite them in
or let me blow snow in at your window,
hear it flake on flake inch up the door.
Or let in this summer wind to rustle
light dry ends of grass up from your stubble floor.

Your First Black Hair

Your first black hair came off
a dark fuzz, half mooned on the sheet
where your head had rubbed.
And in the bath, when I trickled
water over it and smoothed it backwards
from the forehead to the crown

long wet streaks clung to my palm.
Later it was replaced by much lighter
fine brown hair, and though I know
that hair when it leaves the root
is already dead, yours always seemed
extraordinarily alive. And in the womb

hair is the last thing to grow, along with
lashes, eyebrows; things that give the face
definition. Later it will grow
in the warm and secret places of the body
insistent, close, in all the changes that
we go through, scenting us with fear and love.

Your hair grew and changed from light brown to black
although the skin was still too new to shave.
When they cut your long hair off I watched it fall
in a dark half circle on the floor,
your naked face appear. Easy then
to see the line of neck from ear to collar bone,

your throat move as you swallowed.
And now you have the need you no longer
have the time to shave the shadow on
your upper lip as closely as you'd like.
You say you will come back, meanwhile
your hair grows long. I think of the smell

that clings to it that no soap can disguise,
the smell that makes my own hair rise
and leaks, from the close and secret places
of the body, to linger on the sheets I stroke
the way I'd stroke the fur of an animal
the way the thick hair grows.

Crooning

Your father holds you tight,
his mouth next to your ear.
You're wakeful and alert.
You've been awake most of the night.

You listen to his gentle croon,
nonsense, silly words
to some well known tune.
You blink your eyes until

the lids begin to droop.
He's fallen asleep too,
your heads together
the same black

though later yours will turn
to lighter brown,
then for years
I'll watch it darken.

I wake now restless
listen to a creak on the stair
wonder if you hear
a voice singing through the darkness

song being the first thing
that we recognise
and after everything is gone
the last we hear.

You have that impulse
too, his gift
and any words will do
string them together, ad lib

doo be doo de doo.
Your mattress squeaks,
you shift, to a more
comfortable position

sleepless invent tunes
words that fit,
all night under yours hear his
thread of music.

Charms

I try to imagine the house
with you in it again.
Sliding down into your bed
your basket piled with washing
shirts stained with sweat.

Or striding from room to room
singing under your breath
the words of some song
you thought you had forgotten,

and though it may feel strange at first
the house accommodates you.
You know it hasn't altered.
It's you who have changed.
You will learn it again.

Incant them: table, hallway
chair, like the refrain
of that song you knew;
and trace your invisible footprint

stand where you once stood,
gather in the little parts
of you you thought were lost,
see them fly into the air, adhere
to the magnet of your skin,

and pick up the lucky charm
you used to wear round your neck,
warm the leather thong
that lay inside your drawer, cold for months.

The Risen Man

You say your mattress is so thin
it's taken on the shape of your body.
Imprinted, hollows for your shoulders, head
the ribs and pelvis, ankle bone and foot.

Even when you rise from it,
do ordinary things – wash, clean your teeth
replace the brush, hear it click against the glass
pull down an eyelid, examine your skin,
he's still there, your sleeping twin.

At night you fold yourself into him.
Even if you shake your mattress,
he settles there again.

Remember your nose bleeds, how
the copious blood soaked into the mattress.
Even when I scrubbed I only
rubbed it further in to the grain of the cloth.
And here I am still brushing up
your long hairs and flakes of skin.
Similarly you can't shake or brush him off
although you think you might see him
rise like Lazarus, pick the mattress up,
tuck it under one arm and walk.

When I come to meet you and you look up, cough
that nervous cough, examine your wrist
for the watch you haven't got, pull down a cuff,
I see the man half-risen that you think
sleeps in the indentations you have left.

You know you can't leave him now
hand under one cheek, his foot exposed;
you must bring him with you willingly
before you can walk again or sleep peacefully alone.

Allergies

I noticed first a dryness in the skin,
small rough patches on the elbows, midriff,
the soles of your feet.
Then later on your neck and cheeks.
Wool, detergents, milk,
any irritant and you'd break out.
Then the illnesses, magnificent rashes
where others had a few spots.
Small breaks became deeper,
hard cracks, blackened at the edges.
On your heels, between the fingers,
toes; it was painful to walk.
We caked you in creams, oil in the bathwater,
tried different diets, smoothed you clean
with different soaps.
They said you would grow out of it,
all the cracks and breaks would close
and leave just this slight dryness.
But then they say that everything
eventually breaks out.
Toxins rise and settle on the skin.
Impatient then you make the one clean cut
wait for the swift rush.
And here I am holding you together,
massaging you smooth.

Dos-à-Dos

Months we couldn't make love. Weeks
unable to swallow, we'd eaten no real food.
Sometimes I slept as if drugged. Others I'd wake up;
know he was staring at the dark. Could almost hear him think.

I twitch the sheets now back from our twin hollows.
Once more we sleep, go to work, eat.
And once more we meet. At first it was like coming up
after almost drowning. Now more normally

we lie twined or back to back at ease.
I think if I could see us from above we'd look
like something carved, one mound with all the creases smoothed
sleeping dos-à-dos and feet to feet.

We'd be perfectly symmetrical except
for my hand under one cheek and his
turned palm up on the pillow, our faces like something
brought out of the sea. Almost if you looked you'd think

there'd be little pools of water in the hollows,
lichen, seaweed, sand beginning to creep,
both of us immobile in its settling
except for the faint rise and falling of the sheet.

Hindi Urdu Bol Chaal

In the car you put the tape on;
it settles with a little click
cutting off the Radio One DJ.
First silence, then a whirr
'Hindi Urdu Bol Chaal'
– '*Meera naam hei*'

I repeat the words although I can't
remember what they mean.
You struggle with the script,
black curls bound across the page.
You say the roots are Arabic,
Persian, Sanskrit,

and that the problem is
not knowing the end
or the beginning of a phrase. In this script
they all link up. You say that's like
the complex histories of language,
pictorial or narrative. Where to begin?

Khusran and Shirin listen
to stories told by Shirin's handmaids.
A group of Paladins seated by a pool
hug their cloaks against night winds.
Their horses nose uphill, supremely delicate
their nostrils and their hooves.

Their extended prancing forelegs
span the night, the centuries.
You don't hesitate, make headway
with the cursive script. But I'm appalled
at that sheer leap, don't have your perseverance
or your courage practising out loud

in the street, on real people.
I'm more cautious, embarrassed
if a word is wrong or out of place
and then there's all of that inflection
knowing when to speak,
and when to pause.

Lost

Somewhere some time ago, you lost yourself.
You can't say just when but notice how
your outline's altered, how your hair's changed colour.
How can you be turned back into yourself, become
dark haired again and count the ribs under your skin?

You search old photographs for clues
but each time you look and see yourself reborn
into an eight year old, eleven, twelve, nineteen,
it's your son you see poised to step out.
Our sons and daughters leave thinking they're separate

and for a time and for themselves they are.
But they inherit us and as for you
your son is locked into your heart and you can't
release him. Everywhere you look now he appears,
a young child, schoolboy, a heedless young man

what wouldn't you give to bring him back?
Your ribs, your second teeth. How can you be
transformed into your former self, when he
is there already, twinned with your young ghost.

Gibson Copy

I'm upstairs with a headache, flat out on the bed.
The sound of your playing comes through
cracks in the floorboards. From this far away
I almost like it, and it's the one you've waited years for,
the semi-acoustic, *f*-hole, jazz guitar –
the one you blew the back pay on
(pay we had earmarked for other things).
Like the time you went out to buy a bike,
something second hand, that both of us could use,
came back with a new Peugeot, lightweight,
silver grey, ten speed. Or the holiday in France,
the one we could only just afford. And in between
the things we didn't have, things we could do without,
new clothes, proper haircuts, almost anything
for the house. And that's the way we were and are,
holding it together, just about, putting up with,
stretching it, makeshift – the shelf you made,
held up with shaved down clothes pegs, string.
It's amazing how they last – the ramshackle
car that just keeps going – sagging mattress
we both still roll down to the middle.
But that's the way you like to do it,
mostly guess work, playing it by ear, coming back
just when you'd think we couldn't stretch it any more.
And when you sing, eyes closed
bent over your guitar, your voice soft at first,
a murmur that becomes a strong vibrato
you're still improvising, even as we're ready
to join in – the ones we think we know the words to,
Redemption Song, Desperado, Little Wing.

Inheritance

We discuss the name, divide it into syllables
and guess its derivations.
Our daughter says that it's from Norway
and you produce the evidence
finding photographs of blonde cousins,
remembering your brother.

But you are dark and foreign looking
and our daughter has been taken
for something else, Italian or French;
your mother's father they say
was Welsh. So we examine
ancestry, our place in it

and what we know of it and look
for talents in our children,
miracles, and say they are not ours,
only a gift, when the unexpected thing
breaks out. As for your mother
she was as much at home in Lancashire

as she might have been in Wales
taking your father's name. But it's certain
that you're all musical
and your eyes are the same,
the peat brown of hill pools
that despite the weather doesn't change.

When the Moon is Orange

One night when the trees are tall
when those poplars full but light
sway and fan the sky
one summer night
when the sun is almost down
and the moon is orange
when you are driving home
past the dips and rises
where the bushes are most dense
and there is no sound, no sound
except for a white moth that flutters
suddenly across your path and bangs
against the windscreen,
one night my love, my darling
when the valley is dusky and lovely
when it's you, not your father
in the driving seat
and you are coming back
to do the things you must
you'll see without noticing
the dim pale green of the horizon
how it sinks to darker bluer green
those troughs and rises (no need
to count as they slip past
unnoticed as heartbeats),
this curving road that tracks
your landscape, brings you back
to an empty house (your long
hair clipped back, your competent
hands on the wheel) love
think of the full poplars
orange moon, the dusky horizon
as you pause on the threshold
take in snail trails across the carpet, dust
drawers stuffed with unsorted letters
curtains drawn, a fridge humming and empty,
all of us long gone
and you left to do the things
that today I have done.

Geronimo

If you could take the place of that Indian
in the back seat of the car, the one behind
the chief in his top hat, you'd do it –
there'd be you, two unknown braves, Geronimo
at the wheel of his Cadillac; you the romantic
always can see yourself sloughing off your skin
taking on another one with ease.
But be careful of the hand you deal yourself.
Don't offer yourself up, scalped, shriven, clean.
Don't daub your face; these men are serious
and what you know of them pure guesswork.
But not one to read the subtext
you've already done the deed, stripped in, neatly
inserted now between one phantom and the next.
We can hardly see the difference. You've added
feathers, braids – you're still partly tongue in cheek.
But a hex if you transgress against their loves and griefs.
Don't get mixed up in other more complex mythologies.
Don't grin like that, that grin will never stop,
you won't cry out or speak, nothing more
will issue through those teeth. You think you can
still change the image you've become part of,
but you only move when I flick the page.
Their space goes back, yours is all illusion
shimmering like a mirage or a hologram
pulled this way and that between these patterns
of interference and transference.

Birds Fly South

Birds fly south, on lines of barometric pressure.
They travel flyways, Atlantic and Pacific, enormous distances
across oceans, mountain ranges, to Africa, to South
America. In some mythologies
they sleep on the wing
not stopping for food or water.

From great altitudes they scan landscape,
features, hills and rivers; take bearings from
the stars and sun, or are pulled
by the earth's magnetic field.
They travel day and night,
the Arctic Tern performing yearly a round trip
of twenty-three thousand miles.

It's said they're prompted by a shortening
of daylight, food scarce, the weather colder,
but we can only guess at what impels
their urgent flight.

Likewise other baffling phenomena:
fish in shoals that shift as one,
plankton rising from great depths
to the surface, salmon coursing from freshwater
to open seas, or reindeer crossing snowy wastes
summoned by something
they heard that we had not.

The Aborigines who in the Dreamtime sang
their stones into existence have an explanation
as good as any other. They say they walked
and sang to make their landscape visible
and must trace their Dreamlines still, not erase
the created world of God.

So when we sleep and cross our night latitudes
let's dream the birds, sleeping as they navigate.
(It doesn't matter if they dream us or not.)
With one mind they'll up, tremendous flocks,
and fly without diverting

straight to where they sense warmth,
shade where it's needed, water and food in plenty;
calm breeding grounds, some paradise.
Let's dream the birds flying above us
sleeping on the wing,
not stopping for food or water,
Let's dream the birds flying along lines
of barometric pressure
who, when they reach their resting place, sing.

Icarus

Matisse said the best way he knew of catching
colour was to cut it from the solid sheet.
This was after arthritis made his hands
too clumsy for a brush. So he had them painted,
vast areas of cobalt, cerise
strong golden yellow, apple green
and out of them released flowers, birds,
heavy limbed women, fish, seaweed.
Finally Icarus scissored into flight,
buckling and falling, dancing in agony
through a dark blue night, through sunbursts of stars.
He's cut from black that contains all colours.
Night bleeds through him, its weight
seeps through the red hole that is his heart.

Vincent Writes to Theo from the North

So Theo, once more I'm writing to you
from a cooler climate. This one so like
the Borinage with its infinite varieties of grey,
just when I thought I'd left that grey behind –
and yet these evening skies, so startling when
they're clear. I have to spend those nights outside.
People think I'm crazy but I don't give a damn.
I have this hunger that you know is not for food
but for colour, the reds and sonorous deep blues
that strike a note like music. Violet, rose madder
to my eyes are better than a feast. And because I've tried
to express the terrible passions of humanity
by means of red and green I know that cobalt
is divine, carmine similarly. Last night
I came upon a field just cut. It put me in mind
of the wheat field at St Remy, the one I painted
very yellow, very light. Also a line of poplars
very close in colour to the southern cypresses.
I can't get them out of my mind – so dark
and so massive and as beautiful of line
and proportion as an obelisk. One day
I will paint them again. But for now Theo
you must know that it's harder here and colder
so if there can be a little extra this month
that will be delightful; if not
that will be alright too. And for the paints I need –
6 malachite green, 2 cobalt 3 red ochre,
1 ultramarine, 1 ivory black. You understand
how urgently I need them. And remember Theo
that this sacrifice you make is not
for my sake alone but for this thing
that we call art, this painting that is my obsession
but I think might hold some little value.
And for those colours sent already, many thanks,
the flake white especially much needed.
So brother for the rest – I hope that you'll think
to write one of these days. Until then
I am as ever, yours with a handshake,
                                    Vincent.

Proofs

The plate's been burred, the whole of it
minutely pitted so the ink will hold,
and it would print now deepest black.
But with the same intent that brought
the technique from the eighteenth century to now
I'll smooth the image back.
Mezzotint, coming slowly into the light.

Out of the tones, the half tones and the dark,
'nature mort', still life, flowers, chair
a bowl of fruit, a square table top.
I think of how it's like daybreak,
the return from blackness that revoked terra firma,
and how I'll reach
for what was left the night before

to feel that they are solid there, my proofs
as they take shape out of the first paling grey.
And it begins, the intimate decoding
of the universe: a plate, a chair, flowers
where they were
turning from violet to crimson.

Odalisque

You'd think that after this he'd want to have me,
eat me up like so much fruit, a fresh peach or mango.
But you'd be wrong. Before maybe, but not now
not even when I lie here, everything on show.
All he wants is to position elbows, feet
get the angle of the head just so.
Then he's staking all he's got on lemon yellow,
aubergine; his eyes are narrowed
and I'm only so much line and space
or shapes balanced one against the other.
I want to say 'look at my face'
He says he's painted me
just like a mandolin or fruit,
all curves and tender hollows.
That's for this time.
Already I can feel my breasts drooping
crows feet at the corner of my eyes,
thighs mapped with little broken veins.
And how do I know what else he's seen
or what he's making me into.
It won't be always fruit and mandolins.
I've sneaked a look
at all those canvases that face
into the studio's white walls.
And I've seen the originals,
mouldering and dried up pears and mangoes,
lemons, peaches, and I know
that he can't ever eat them and can't let them go.

Wide Open

After visiting my father we drive back to the hills.
Two and a half hours to reach the hospital.
Now taking the right road
less than half that time to travel home.

As we reach the hills it starts to rain.
The headlights swing and shine
We're on the last lap of the climb
out of the valley. Somewhere above, the sky

is opening. You push a tape in
as we lift into emptiness and cloud.
Tom Petty and the Heartbreakers.
You turn the tape up very loud.

My Father's Teeth

The hospital again; they've lost my father's teeth.
I ring them to protest. Without his teeth
he can't eat. They say they'll give him Complan,
have him measured for another set.
I know this could take weeks.

Meanwhile I can't understand a word he says.
They say, no need, they can interpret.
I say without his teeth he can't sing or whistle.
They say he doesn't want to, anyway
he has his radio and he can *listen*.

I want to say, without his teeth his mouth caves in;
I hardly recognise him. They say it's not as if
those teeth were his own. I know,
but they've filled his mouth for years
and he's still looking for them, under the bed,

bedside cupboard, pockets of his pyjamas.
I help him in this fruitless search.
The teeth are gone. I imagine how
they might have taken on another life,
laughing, saying things he said, biting into

sandwiches, pork pies, having bits picked out with
a sharpened matchstick; singing, whistling out loud.
Even if we found them now, they'd not be his,
wouldn't fit. His face is shrivelling and although
he's cheerful, his mouth is stretched

in an eerie smile. I think of how eventually
everything is lost, those things by which
we know ourselves; eyes and eyebrows, nose,
the whorls on the fingertips, and done with then
the power of speech, of sight, hearing, where we fit

in the scheme of things; family, relationships.
He shakes his head. I think I hear
the lost teeth click, top against the bottom,

inside his clothes, the clinkered bone
rub against bone; no way to build them up again –

the eyes, the mouth, the head, or resurrect
the bonnie flesh. What's left, this rattle
and dry susurration, when side by side
we come to rest and all the other things
we knew each other by are gone.

Six Foot

You've reached six foot, caught up and overshot
your father by a good few inches – me
by a whole twelve. I note this with relief
as if the height you'd reached gave you
a guarantee, as if your head up there
where I can hardly reach had made you less
not more vulnerable. I should have understood
your height would make me helpless –
there was the accident I rushed back to
dry mouthed, convinced that it was you
and not daring to imagine any detail –
when they said 'they pulled him out, covered his head'
I would not picture it. To imagine
anything is to ill-wish; to predict
is to bespeak the deed – so stop at this –
you were not him. What happens next,
the catch released, the spring, the hood
peeled back – your grin, your eyes opened
and we imagine nothing evil, nothing good,
let things follow their natural progress
as you unscathed step out to how it should
go on, to what it comes down to; that's you
six foot above, me six foot underground.

Early Warning

You used to wake to find yourself
in a strange bed and not turn a hair.
A stranger's face in close up touching yours,
a pillow dented to an unfamiliar shape,
early mornings, an unfamiliar room.

You had them taped, the casual relationships.
Even so you chose with care,
smoothing an eyebrow in the mirror
you could smile, adjust your tie, the rings
you could afford to wear, the gold cufflinks.

You loved the city nights, awake till the small hours.
You thought you were intact
eyes and skin still clear
muscles and sinews tight.
Where were they then, your early warnings?

You could take them all. Jobs in hotels
late nights, alcohol
catnaps at the desk
or long hours at a stretch
afternoons in darkened bedsits.

And you said you didn't dream. Now
when I ask you say you do.
And do you dream in colour?
Yes – intense, polychrome; violet, green
deep midnight blue and acid yellow.

You dream your childhood.
You dream the seasons; summer, autumn
the unbearable gold, you dream
the winter's cold, you dream your death
and each time it's different

although in dreams at least you always
know yourself. Now when you wake alone
exhausted in the tangled sheets

your body drips. Your fingers search –
the soles of your feet, armpits dried to salt,

the skin in folds around your midriff.
At your wrist the bones show through.
You look for lesions, the defences
of your body breached, your tongue
in the mirror furred; an old man's face.

But you know it by the gold fillings
in the teeth. You look back for the onset
of the disease. Were you whole once?
You wake and sleep and wake, wait
for the next fever coming on.

Each Star is a Sun

Although we know that each star is sun, we call them stars.
And though the glass whose rim we run our fingers round
is spun and fused from sand; though water not heat
wears sand down and glass shatters when its rim is rung
we trust glass to drink from, sand to walk across
and not wear down, the stars to come out.

And though we know that booming sound inside a shell
that we say is the sea, is just an echo made
by any enclosed space against our eardrum,
the beating we say is our own blood, our hearts
can be another one's. We hear it magnified
when the womb expands or when we hold someone.

And glass shatters to vibrations from your guitar's
plucked string, not from the high pitched sound
they say is wrung from galaxies. The planets pulse
although they have no light of their own, give back
the sun's reflection; and when they swing
it's only an apparent shift in their position. They come

Orion, Aldebaran, the Winter Hexagon,
wanderers sometimes that dazzle us.
Look up, light's travelling to us still,
heat from this yellow star we call a sun.

Lagoon

The water of this Adriatic coast
is clear; warm and green. Almost
you could see down to the bottom.
You watch him float then plunge
out of the sun, the jewelled skin
when he comes up again
shaking off the drops. He rests his chin
on the edge of the li-lo, idles in the heat
of the late afternoon. You watch
eyes narrowed to the glare, thinking of
your native cold dark water. Even here
you hate to be engulfed or see him disappear
even for a second, remembering the story
of the boy out for the day (it was
his first step in the water), swept under
by a giant wave and never seen again. And not just
his story but also what you see,
that there's nothing so completely strange
as this other element; how in it things change shape
transform and if they don't dissolve or break
may be ground down by the infinite resources of the sea.
And you don't want to be that woman
one hand to her cheek, searching urgently
for a dark shape in the water. So
you call him in at last, hold him in
a rough towel, rub him dry, rub
away the glitter of drops, the stubborn sand.

Sunburn

All summer you stay pale, keep out of the sun.
Your skin so white, the blue veins are a shock.
Out of the glare of the afternoon
I check you're there – minutes to adjust
to the dim room where you've taken refuge.

Pale and fractious most of that holiday
you stayed inside. Even on the beach
you kept under a shade, waved the camera away.
But when the film unspooled, slowly
in another dark back bedroom

you came up again, startlingly white
as if the sun had searched you out,
lit your bones to brilliance, predicted
your ghost. You're fixed, a child's phantom
teeth bared, gesticulating, the glowing

skull that I confused with stories of your head
seared by the radium. But the whiteness
proved you were there; gave you substance
when we'd been afraid that only rectangles of black
would float up in the shallow tray.

Test

Alone you leave the test card on.
Even when you're upstairs, the screen
filling the house. You hear the faint drone
making the house breathe with something
like life. It flickers, a giant coloured image
and you breathe back on it, use it to check
your make-up, teeth. In the screen your skin
keeps the illusion of a tan much stronger
than a mirror. You think of the test
for amber, how the sun magnified
shines through the yellow substance, hooks
on the small creature caught inside. And you think
of the slide test for this other small thing
lately identified that grows to suck in your whole world.

Mr Wrong

Time after time we came but the place was always empty.
We knew it well enough,
the first time galloping up
horses in a sweat – we held them until we had to drop
the reins; sliding off at the gate, the smell
of clothes we'd worn all night.
That was when we cut the way through.
Luckily we had thick leather gloves
tough boots. But the briars were strong – just
gone winter, thorns black on the ropey stalks.
Six of us to hack our way past them,
one tore at my face. I still have the long scar,
blood studded it then, the whole length
dried to the colour of juice from damsons.
The next time the path still there and we got further;
and again when we came back,
this time roaring up, oil on our boots, the engines hot
and the men raucous – they'd drunk too much
but they became silent as we stooped through the briar tunnel.
It hadn't grown over but seemed gloomier.
We fell in with the quiet around us, laughing nervous
after the uprush of pigeons which we took for a sign.
But that was all, no living body
nothing asleep, not even a footprint in the dust.
And now the men won't come, but I keep returning
to this staircase, this room, convinced I'll see
the flick of a hem disappearing round a door,
certain that I'll hear faint music.
So this is what I have to do, just keep
waiting here, wiping my breath from the mirror
practising a kiss.

Betrayal

The twitch betrays you, coming back after all those years
of thinking it had disappeared.
You squeeze your eyes together, shake your head
and everything that you had taken on
just falls away; they say
old habits die hard, like loves

and here's the proof of it that comes
from the pit of the stomach
up; that surge
that's like a battery recharged.

And after so much time apart
we thought all that was done, the past
buried, but there's the face behind
the face you'd schooled to give nothing away
rising to the surface – mine
likewise is stripped

and so that's both of us naked
both of us betrayed
by the thing we thought was dead
jump-starting into life again.

The Sign For Water

He makes the sign for water.
She makes the sign for fish.
His movement fluid from the shoulder.
Hers swifter, starting from the wrist,

thumb uppermost, cutting the air
like the quick flick-tailing fish
through water. They meet;
his hands slide over hers

and it's there almost as if he'd drawn
the three lines of the hieroglyph
that we know denote.liquid,
ocean, waves. And as she draws

the letters on his palm and he
makes out the word-shape with his lips
the whole hydraulic motion of the earth
rolls under them.

So my deaf child speaks
to his lover, without sound,
hands closing the air between her meaning
and his profound lack of hearing.

He crosses both his hands
over the place he knows
his heart to be, and when he holds
the cupped palms out then we

expect to see it pulse
between them. They'll touch and speak
like this all their lives,
his lover, my deaf child

their mutual dialogue
silent and complete. Their love's
language has no rules.
They leap it as the silver

leaping fish. What are they talking about
now? Miracles or loaves,
it doesn't matter as he makes the sign for fish
and she makes the sign for water.

Sign Language

The eldest child, my brother, was profoundly deaf.
At two, hearing tests confirmed, the loss had been
complete, although at first you wouldn't guess
our languages were different. Signs or speech,

we moved between them easily enough
We knew that we must touch his shoulder,
cheek, and turn his face towards us
before we spoke. And he was quicker

than we were at other things. Games
that needed sharp eyes, good balance.
His body primed and tuned, to outweigh
his sleeping ears. And though just then

there seemed no difference between us,
looking back the difference is plain.
I see how well the camera has caught him,
not smiling as we did but puzzling as if

intensity of observation
could make up for the faculty he lacked.
Now miles away we can't make the signs
as fluently. But, bones, hair, skin

we resemble one another. Sometimes in dreams
I part cool waves and hear his whisper
audible and clear as waking it could never be.
And he is there, his fingers move like seaweed,

his hair fronds out, his head swings like a dead man's.
I touch his cold green lips, the shuttered lids
and hardly recognise the face; but it is his.
He opens those hyacinth blue eyes and I'm

caught, inhabiting the same closed element
that he does. I'm dumb. My hands slip from him.
When I wake I'm alone. Decades have gone
and we speak a different language. But he

still slumbers with me. At night at rest
like any other a confederacy of sleep
conceals his deafness. You wouldn't guess
what soundless dreams might stir his bed.

Collector

The sea curls its way in
along this coast; we stop
late afternoon to watch
the sun on white sailed boats.

Intent and serious your girl
searches for stones and shells.
Her boots laced together, slung
around her neck are filled.

Her hands have sifted
curiously shaped pebbles
dried star fish,
her trouser hems are stained with salt.

Imagine how much later
in her room
she will bend down,
her hair will fall across her cheek.

Imagine how she will
unroll her jeans
and they will trickle out
small heaps of dry sand.

Fluke

You thought it would come out, despite everything
the way you've heard it happens sometimes;
the device overruled; the insistent egg
tenacious, unwilling to move and you
willing it to grow, limbs, eyebrows.
The ring just something to trawl through.
You imagined the silent swimming;
the forearms and the little webbed hands,
and the ring not plastic after all
but glowing and golden. You imagined it
despite everything, despite the blood
which you hoped wouldn't be the thing it was,
but a proof of living. And just as you have heard
it can happen sometimes – the marvellous fluke
heaved out, into the open, whole and smiling,
the child with the coil in its hand.

One Man and his Dog

Saturday, late morning, hardly light; it's been raining
steadily all night. Downstairs the dog is keening
that noise in his throat you can't ignore
although your head's heavy, your tongue furred
already you have one foot on the floor,
already you have one hand at the door.
You stumble over piles of newspapers and curse.
The dog is whining louder as you come downstairs,
keep coming down, you know that state
half dreaming when you think you are awake.

And this is no dog as old as you in human years
but a young wire haired fox terrier
and you're crouched one hand on his collar
the other curled into the springy fur.
His hot breath is on your face, his tongue
and now you can't remember how the dog you lost
became the dog who brushed his tail against your leg
the dog who sleeps now on your bed
that's not the border cross whose black and white
slipped before you in the half light.

This dog has pressed his narrow shape under the fence.
He's a shadow at the bridge that when you look again
is gone, and you haven't learnt the trick of whistling
him back yet, like the greyhound you watched streaking
over open moorland –
the long silence that you knew was wrong,
the dog you carried two miles home
not sure who was trembling the most.

Don't let them say those eyes can't follow you
or that he didn't know, the same dog who
knew every road to every pub, the dog
who was yours or your father's; that dog
keening is the same as that dog in the rain, the one
whose place on the floor you scrubbed, the one
whose rug you shook and threw away, the dog
you wept for, well it was okay then to weep for a dog.

Night Swimmers

They do the easy glide across the roof –
night swimmers, impervious, aloof
and assured as seals. From the dark outside
we see the blue reflection heave,
their close formations ripple down the pool.
When they're done, shaking drops
from arms and legs, hair fanned out;
the roof is still unsettled
fluid with the slip and slop of water
against tiles or as if it's shaken
by its own disordered molecules.
We listen ears acute, as if we could tell
the sound that glass might make
reverting to its liquid state; or as if
the night might echo with that booming sound
the way the sea seems to resound inside a shell.